DAILY GRATITUDE JOURNAL

FOR KIDS

THIS JOURNAL BELONGS TO

....

DAY: _____   **DATE:** ____ / ____ / ____

I MADE SOMEONE SMILE TODAY WHEN...

THIS WAS THE FUNNIEST MOMENT OF THE DAY...

DRAW OR
WRITE HERE

WHAT
DID YOU DO?

TODAY, I MOSTLY FELT...

 **TODAY, I AM MOST THANKFUL FOR...**

_____

_____

_____

DAY: _____   DATE: ____ / ____ / ____

SOMETHING KIND SOMEONE
SAID TO ME
TODAY...

THE ANIMAL I AM MOST
THANKFUL FOR...

DRAW IT HERE

WRITE WHAT
THEY SAID

WHAT ARE YOU MOST
GRATEFUL FOR TODAY?

_____

_____

_____

_____

RATE THE DAY

GREAT!

OK

NOT SO GREAT!

DAY: _____   **DATE:** _____ / _____ / _____

I WAS PROUD OF MYSELF TODAY WHEN...

WHAT TASTE ARE YOU MOST GRATEFUL FOR?

WHAT DID YOU DO?

DRAW OR WRITE HERE

RATE THE DAY

☆ ☆ ☆ ☆ ☆

 **SOMETHING I AM THANKFUL FOR TODAY...**

_____

_____

_____

DAY: _____   **DATE:** ____ / ____ / ____

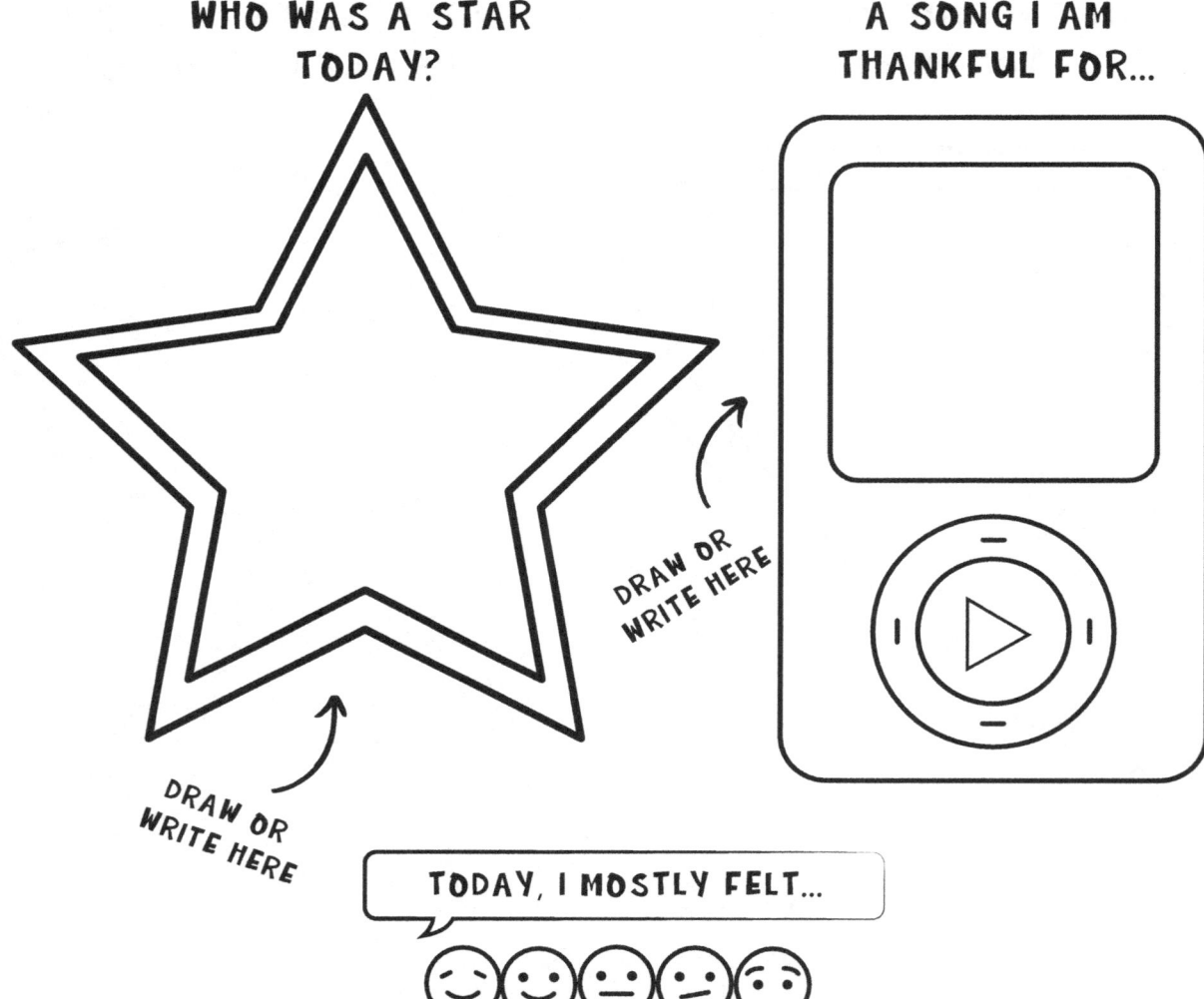

WHO WAS A STAR
TODAY?

A SONG I AM
THANKFUL FOR...

DRAW OR
WRITE HERE

DRAW OR
WRITE HERE

TODAY, I MOSTLY FELT...

➡ TODAY, I AM MOST GRATEFUL FOR...

_____

_____

_____

DAY: _____

DATE: _____ / _____ / _____

I WAS A GOOD FRIEND TODAY WHEN...

WHAT DID YOU DO?

WHICH GIFT ARE YOU MOST GRATEFUL FOR?

WHAT ARE YOU MOST THANKFUL FOR TODAY?

_____

_____

_____

_____

DRAW OR WRITE HERE

RATE THE DAY

GREAT!

OK

NOT SO GREAT!

DAY: _____   **DATE:** ___ / ___ / ___

SOMEONE WHO IS ALWAYS THERE FOR ME...

DRAW THEM HERE

THE BEST THING ABOUT MY ROOM IS...

DRAW OR WRITE HERE

RATE THE DAY

♡ ♡ ♡ ♡ ♡

WHAT WERE YOU MOST GRATEFUL FOR THIS WEEK?

_____

_____

_____

DAY: _____   DATE: /   /

I AM SO GRATEFUL I
KNOW HOW TO...

THE HOBBY I AM MOST
GRATEFUL FOR IS...

DRAW OR
WRITE HERE

TODAY, I MOSTLY FELT...

DRAW OR
WRITE HERE

SOMETHING I AM LOOKING FORWARD TO NEXT WEEK...

_____

_____

_____

DAY: _____

DATE: ____ / ____ / ____

I MADE SOMEONE LAUGH TODAY WHEN...

THE PEOPLE I AM MOST GRATEFUL FOR...

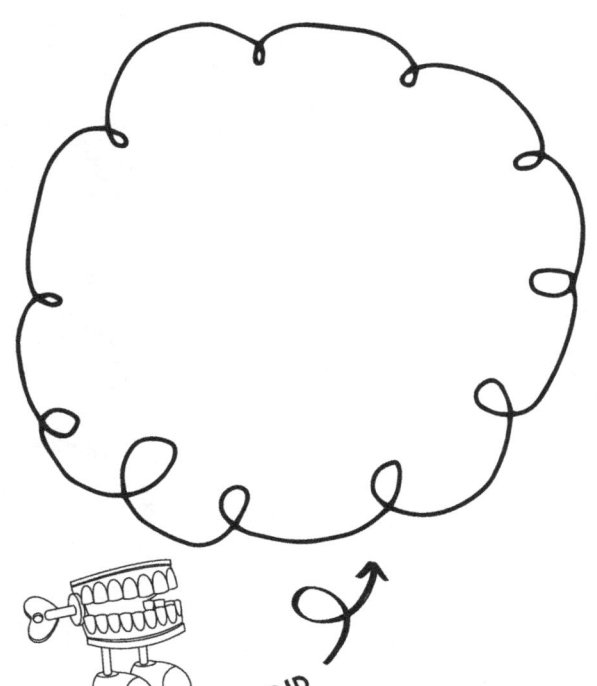

WHAT DID YOU DO?

DRAW THEM HERE

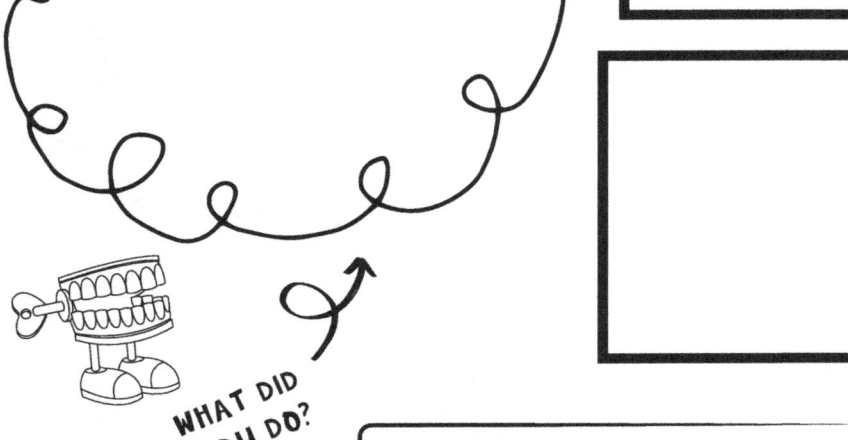

TODAY, I MOSTLY FELT...

 **TODAY, I AM MOST THANKFUL FOR...**

_____

_____

_____

DAY: _____   DATE: _____ / _____ / _____

I TRIED HARD TODAY WHEN...

THE HAPPIEST MOMENT OF THE DAY WAS...

DRAW OR WRITE HERE

DRAW OR WRITE HERE

WHAT ARE YOU MOST GRATEFUL FOR TODAY?

_____

_____

_____

_____

RATE THE DAY

| 10 |
| 9 |
| 8 |
| 7 |
| 6 |
| 5 |
| 4 |
| 3 |
| 2 |
| 1 |
| 0 |

10 ← GREAT!

5 ← OK

1
0 ← NOT SO GREAT!

DAY: _____ **DATE:** ___ / ___ / ___

TODAY'S AWARD FOR KINDNESS GOES TO...

WHICH MEAL WERE YOU MOST GRATEFUL FOR TODAY?

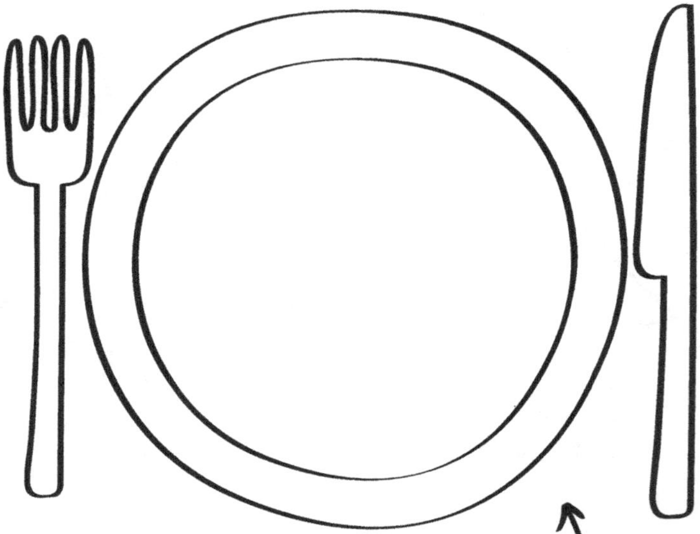

DRAW OR WRITE HERE

DRAW OR WRITE HERE

RATE THE DAY

✓ ✓ ✓ ✓ ✓

 **SOMETHING I AM THANKFUL FOR TODAY...**

_____

_____

_____

DAY: _____

DATE: ___ / ___ / ___

I WAS HELPFUL TODAY WHEN...

WHAT DID YOU DO? ↱

WHAT PUT A SMILE ON YOUR FACE TODAY?

DRAW OR WRITE HERE ↰

TODAY, I MOSTLY FELT...

➡ **TODAY, I AM MOST GRATEFUL FOR...**

_____

_____

_____

DAY: _____   **DATE:** ___ / ___ / ___

I FELT CONFIDENT TODAY WHEN...

WHICH VEHICLE ARE YOU MOST GRATEFUL FOR?

DRAW OR WRITE HERE

DRAW OR WRITE HERE

WHAT ARE YOU MOST THANKFUL FOR TODAY?

_____

_____

_____

_____

RATE THE DAY

GREAT!

OK

NOT SO GREAT!

DAY: _____

DATE: ___ / ___ / ___

WHO DID SOMETHING NICE FOR YOU TODAY?

DRAW THEM HERE

SOMETHING I ENJOY DOING INDOORS...

DRAW OR WRITE HERE

RATE THE DAY

WHAT WERE YOU MOST GRATEFUL FOR THIS WEEK?

_____

_____

_____

DAY: _____

DATE: ____ / ____ / ____

I FELT CARED ABOUT TODAY WHEN...

DRAW OR
WRITE HERE

THE TALENT I AM MOST GRATEFUL FOR IS...

DRAW OR
WRITE HERE

TODAY, I MOSTLY FELT...

☆ SOMETHING I AM LOOKING FORWARD TO NEXT WEEK... ☆

☆ _____ ☆

_____

☆ _____ ☆

DAY: _____   DATE: /   /

I LISTENED TO SOMEONE TODAY WHEN...

THE BEST THING ABOUT THE MORNING IS...

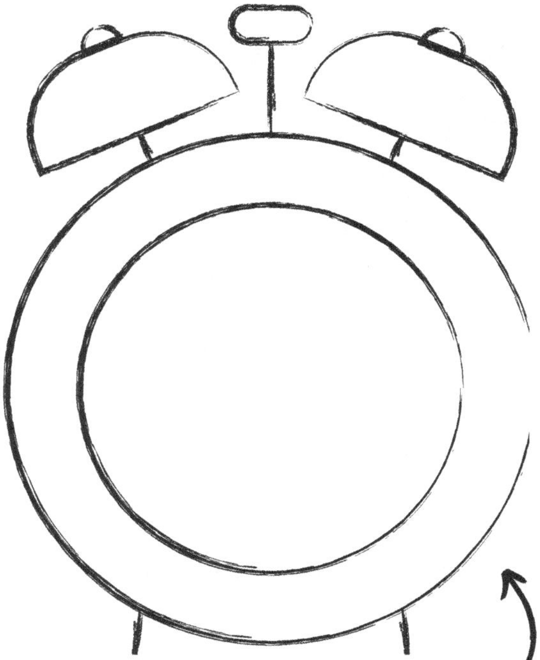

DRAW OR WRITE HERE

DRAW OR WRITE HERE

TODAY, I MOSTLY FELT...

 TODAY, I AM MOST THANKFUL FOR...

_____

_____

_____

DAY: _____ DATE: ___/___/___

SOMEONE MADE ME GIGGLE TODAY WHEN...

THE THING I LOVE MOST ABOUT THE PLANET IS...

WHAT DID THEY DO?

DRAW OR WRITE HERE

WHAT ARE YOU MOST GRATEFUL FOR TODAY?

_____

_____

_____

_____

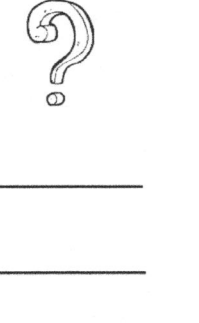

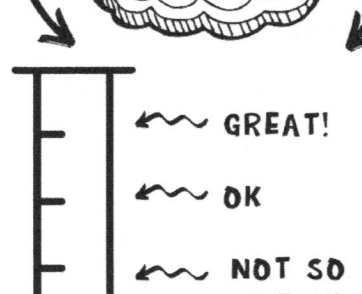

RATE THE DAY

↙ GREAT!

↙ OK

↙ NOT SO GREAT!

DAY: _____   DATE: /   /

I SOLVED A PROBLEM TODAY WHEN...

THE BEST THING ABOUT SCHOOL IS...

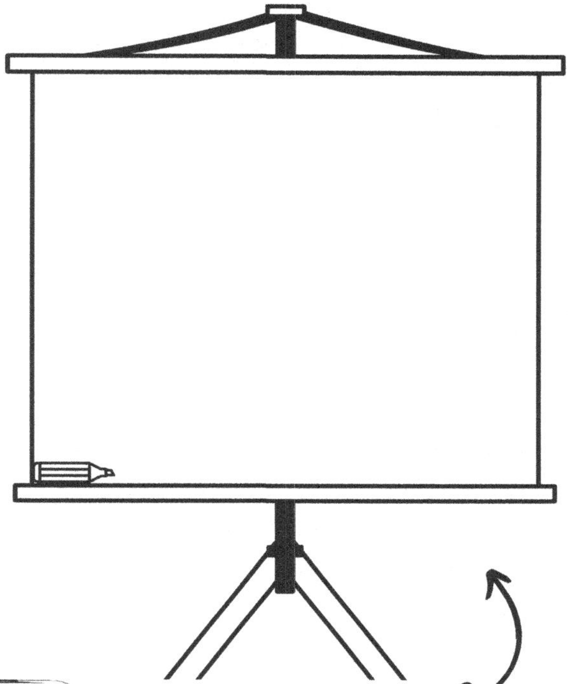

WHAT DID YOU DO?

DRAW OR WRITE HERE

RATE THE DAY

☆ ☆ ☆ ☆ ☆

 SOMETHING I AM THANKFUL FOR TODAY...

_____

_____

_____

DAY: _____   **DATE:** ____ / ____ / ____

WHO THANKED YOU TODAY?

THANK YOU!

A RELATIVE I AM THANKFUL FOR...

DRAW OR WRITE HERE

TODAY, I MOSTLY FELT...

DRAW THEM HERE

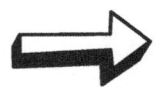

TODAY, I AM MOST GRATEFUL FOR...

_____

_____

_____

DAY: _____   DATE: ___ / ___ / ___

SOMETHING NICE I SAID
TO SOMEONE TODAY...

A TV SHOW I AM
GRATEFUL FOR...

WHAT DID
YOU SAY?

DRAW OR
WRITE HERE

WHAT ARE YOU MOST
THANKFUL FOR TODAY?

RATE THE
DAY

_____

_____

_____

_____

GREAT!

OK

NOT SO
GREAT!

DAY: _____ **DATE:** ___ / ___ / ___

WHO MADE YOU FEEL SPECIAL TODAY?

SOMETHING IN MY HOUSE I AM GRATEFUL FOR...

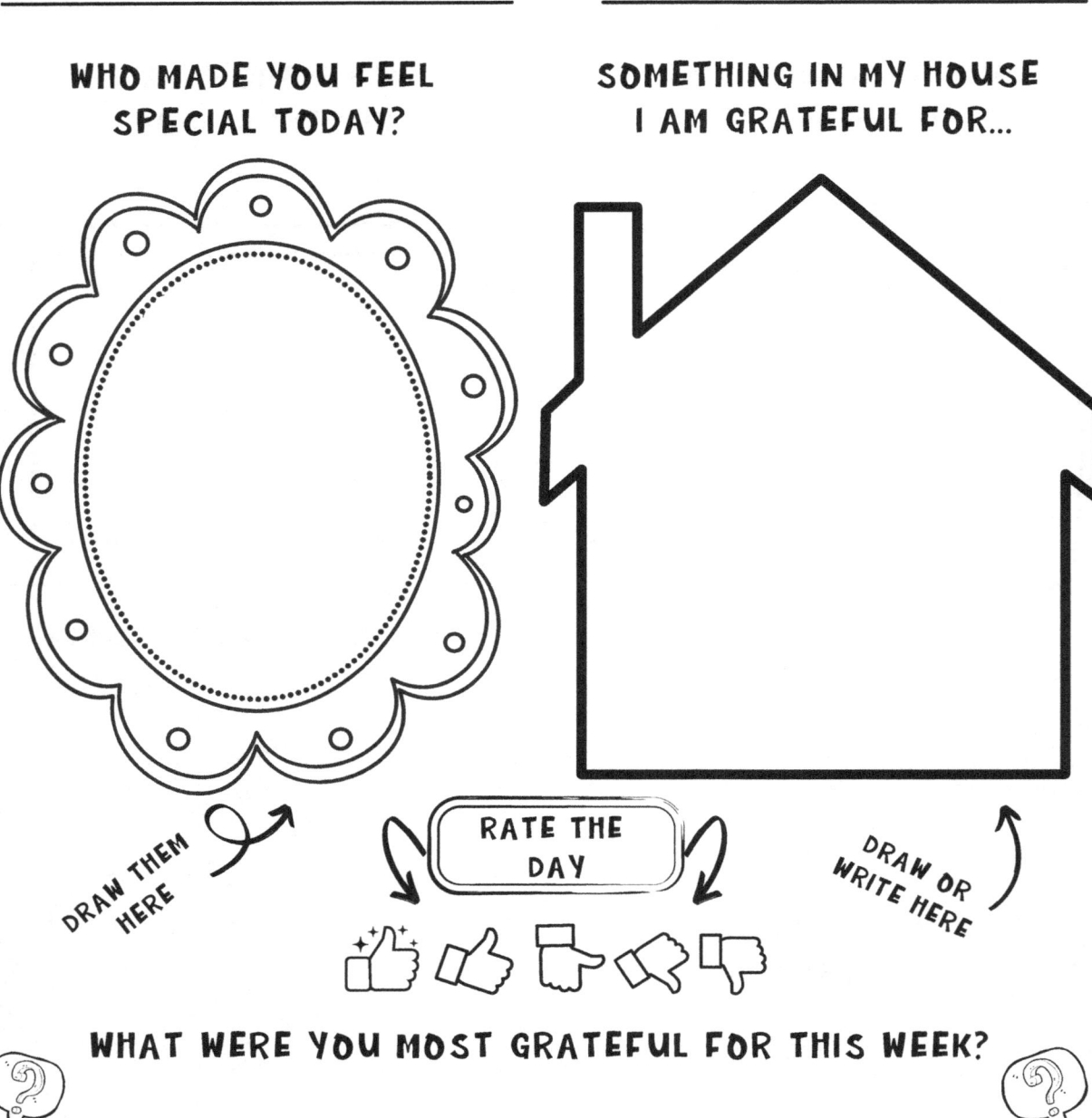

DRAW THEM HERE

RATE THE DAY

DRAW OR WRITE HERE

WHAT WERE YOU MOST GRATEFUL FOR THIS WEEK?

_____

_____

_____

DAY: _____   DATE: ___ / ___ / ___

I WAS EXCITED TODAY
WHEN...

WHICH ONE OF YOUR SENSES
ARE YOU MOST GRATEFUL
FOR TODAY?

DRAW OR
WRITE HERE

SHADE IT
IN

TODAY, I MOSTLY FELT...

☆ SOMETHING I AM LOOKING FORWARD TO NEXT WEEK... ☆

☆ _____

_____

☆ _____

DAY: _____   DATE: _____ / _____ / _____

I WAS THOUGHTFUL TODAY WHEN...

WHAT DID YOU DO?

THE BEST THING ABOUT MEETING NEW PEOPLE IS...

DRAW OR WRITE HERE

TODAY, I MOSTLY FELT...

TODAY, I AM MOST THANKFUL FOR...

_____

_____

_____

DAY: _____   **DATE:** ___ / ___ / ___

I FELT INCLUDED TODAY WHEN...

SOMETHING I ENJOYED MAKING...

DRAW IT HERE

DRAW OR WRITE HERE

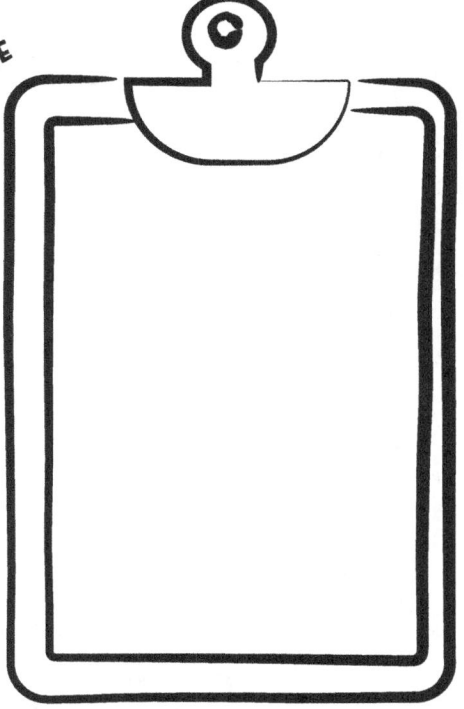

WHAT ARE YOU MOST GRATEFUL FOR TODAY?

_____

_____

_____

_____

RATE THE DAY

~ GREAT!

~ OK

~ NOT SO GREAT!

DAY: _____

DATE: _____ / _____ / _____

WHO MADE YOU FEEL IMPORTANT TODAY?

THE BEST THING ABOUT THE UNIVERSE IS...

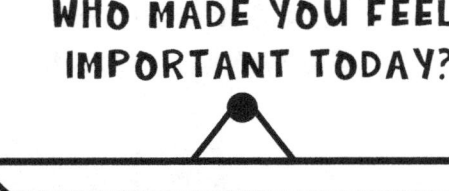

DRAW THEM HERE

RATE THE DAY

DRAW OR WRITE HERE

SOMETHING I AM THANKFUL FOR TODAY...

_____

_____

_____

DAY: _____   **DATE:** ____ / ____ / ____

TODAY, I ENJOYED SPENDING TIME WITH...   **A BOOK I AM THANKFUL FOR...**

DRAW OR WRITE HERE   DRAW OR WRITE HERE

TODAY, I MOSTLY FELT...

TODAY, I AM MOST GRATEFUL FOR...

_____

_____

_____

DAY: _____ DATE: ___/___/___

I FELT HAPPY TODAY WHEN...

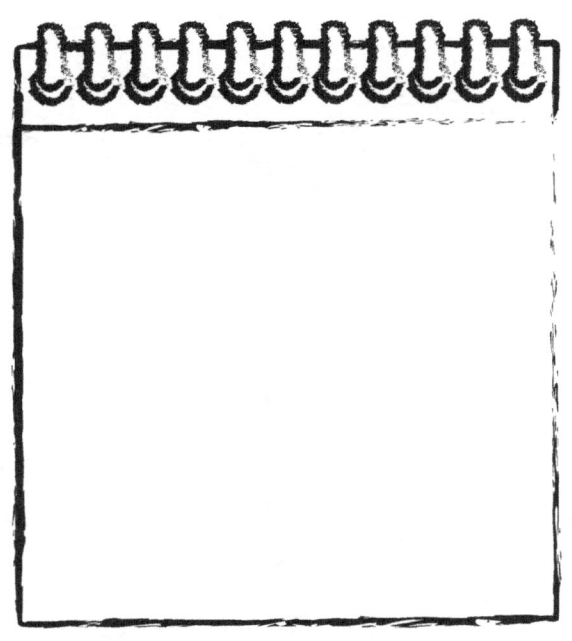

WHICH SNACK ARE YOU MOST GRATEFUL FOR?

DRAW OR WRITE HERE

 WHAT ARE YOU MOST THANKFUL FOR TODAY?

_____

_____

_____

_____

RATE THE DAY

10	← GREAT!
9	
8	
7	
6	
5	← OK
4	
3	
2	
1	← NOT SO
0	← GREAT!

DAY: _____

DATE: _____ / _____ / _____

SOMETHING THOUGHTFUL SOMEONE DID FOR ME TODAY...

THE HAPPIEST DAY OF MY LIFE SO FAR WAS...

WHAT DID THEY DO?

DRAW OR WRITE HERE

RATE THE DAY

WHAT WERE YOU MOST GRATEFUL FOR THIS WEEK?

_____

_____

_____

DAY: _____ **DATE:** ___ / ___ / ___

I ENJOYED DOING THIS TODAY...

THE THING I LOVE MOST ABOUT MYSELF...

↰ DRAW OR WRITE HERE

DRAW OR WRITE HERE

TODAY, I MOSTLY FELT...

☆ **SOMETHING I AM LOOKING FORWARD TO NEXT WEEK...** ☆

☆ _____ ☆

_____

☆ _____ ☆

DAY: _____ **DATE:** ____ / ____ / ____

SOMETHING KIND I SAID TO SOMEONE TODAY...

THE BEST THING ABOUT LUNCHTIME IS...

WHAT DID YOU SAY?

DRAW OR WRITE HERE

TODAY, I MOSTLY FELT...

 **TODAY, I AM MOST THANKFUL FOR...**

_____

_____

_____

DAY: _____

WHO MADE YOU FEEL HAPPY TODAY?

THE WEATHER I AM MOST THANKFUL FOR...

DRAW IT HERE

DRAW THEM HERE

WHAT ARE YOU MOST GRATEFUL FOR TODAY?

RATE THE DAY

GREAT!

OK

NOT SO GREAT!

_____

_____

_____

_____

DAY: _____

DATE: ___ / ___ / ___

I WAS BRAVE TODAY WHEN...

WHAT DID YOU DO?

THE INVENTION I AM MOST GRATEFUL FOR...

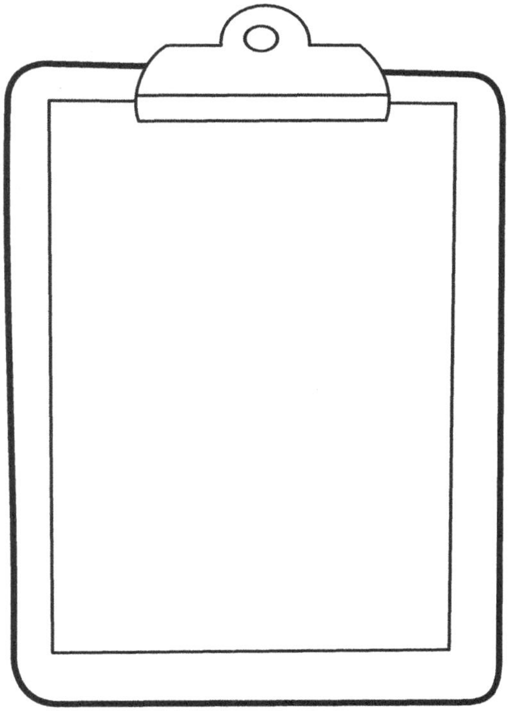

DRAW OR WRITE HERE

RATE THE DAY

☆ ☆ ☆ ☆ ☆

 **SOMETHING I AM THANKFUL FOR TODAY...**

_____

_____

_____

DAY: _____   DATE: ___ / ___ / ___

SOMETHING TINY I AM
GRATEFUL FOR...

THE LESSON I ENJOY
THE MOST IS...

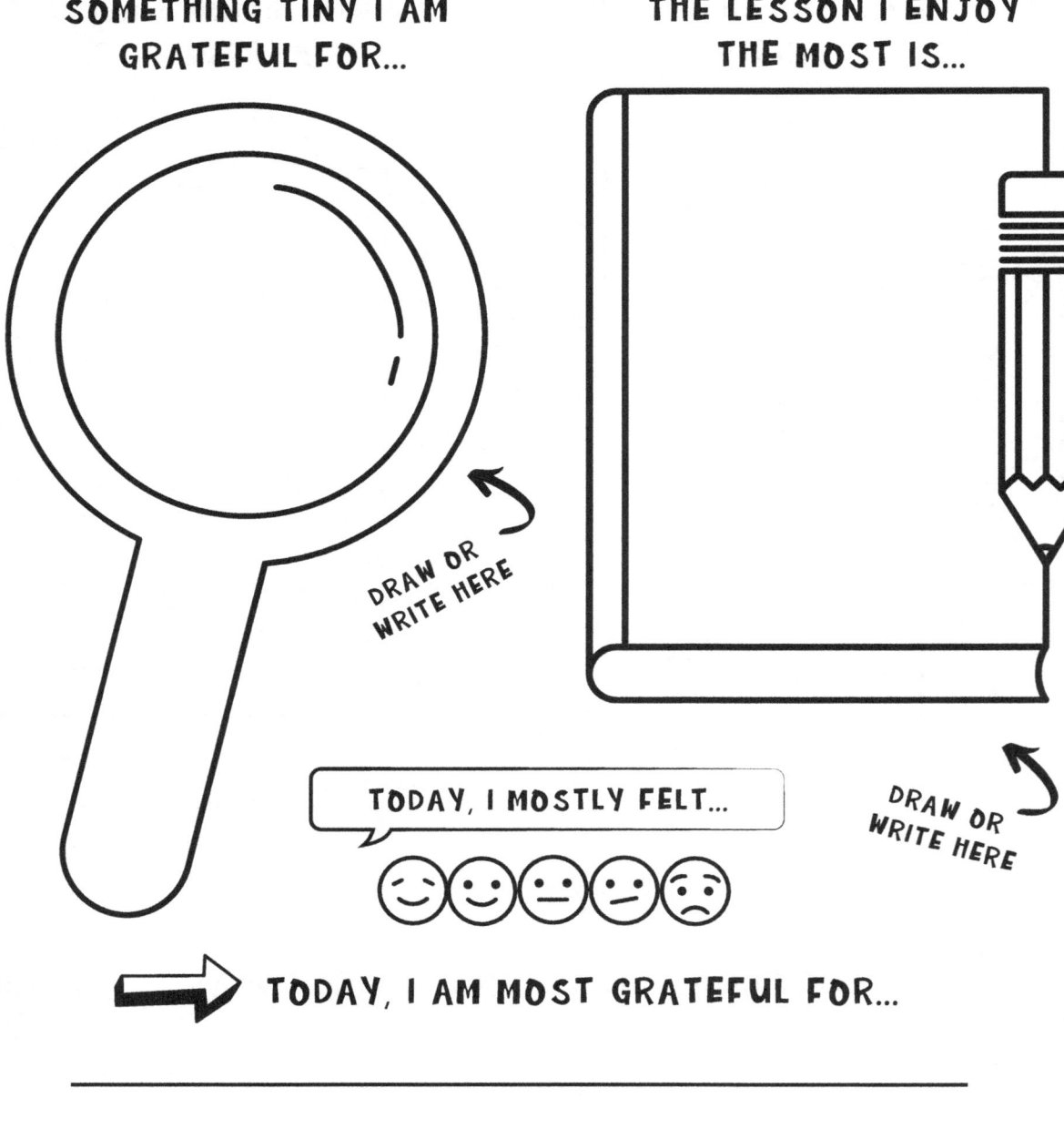

DRAW OR
WRITE HERE

DRAW OR
WRITE HERE

TODAY, I MOSTLY FELT...

TODAY, I AM MOST GRATEFUL FOR...

_____

_____

_____

DAY: _____

DATE: ___ / ___ / ___

I THANKED SOMEONE TODAY WHEN...

DRAW OR WRITE HERE

SOMETHING I ALWAYS ENJOY DOING...

DRAW OR WRITE HERE

WHAT ARE YOU MOST THANKFUL FOR TODAY?

_____

_____

_____

_____

RATE THE DAY

← GREAT!

← OK

← NOT SO GREAT!

DAY: _____ DATE: _____ / _____ / _____

WHO MADE YOU FEEL SAFE TODAY?

MY BEST BIRTHDAY SO FAR WAS...

DRAW THEM HERE

RATE THE DAY

DRAW OR WRITE HERE

WHAT WERE YOU MOST GRATEFUL FOR THIS WEEK?

DAY: _____

DATE: _____ / _____ / _____

I AM SO GRATEFUL I CAN DO...

WHICH ITEM OF CLOTHING ARE YOU MOST THANKFUL FOR TODAY?

DRAW OR WRITE HERE

DRAW IT HERE

TODAY, I MOSTLY FELT...

☆ **SOMETHING I AM LOOKING FORWARD TO NEXT WEEK...** ☆

☆ _____

_____

☆ _____ ☆

DAY: _____   **DATE:** ____ / ____ / ____

I MADE SOMEONE FEEL CARED FOR TODAY WHEN...

A PERSON I AM GLAD TO HAVE IN MY LIFE...

WHAT DID YOU DO?

DRAW THEM HERE

TODAY, I MOSTLY FELT...

 **TODAY, I AM MOST THANKFUL FOR...**

_____

_____

_____

DAY: _____

DATE: _____ / _____ / _____

I FELT LUCKY TODAY WHEN...

WHAT HAPPENED?

WHICH SPORT ARE YOU MOST THANKFUL FOR?

DRAW OR WRITE HERE

WHAT ARE YOU MOST GRATEFUL FOR TODAY?

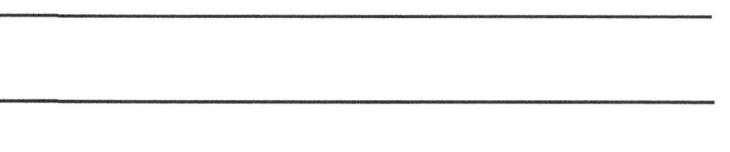

_____

_____

_____

_____

RATE THE DAY

← GREAT!

← OK

← NOT SO GREAT!

DAY: _____ **DATE:** ____ / ____ / ____

WHO MADE YOU SMILE TODAY?

WHICH SOUND ARE YOU MOST GRATEFUL FOR?

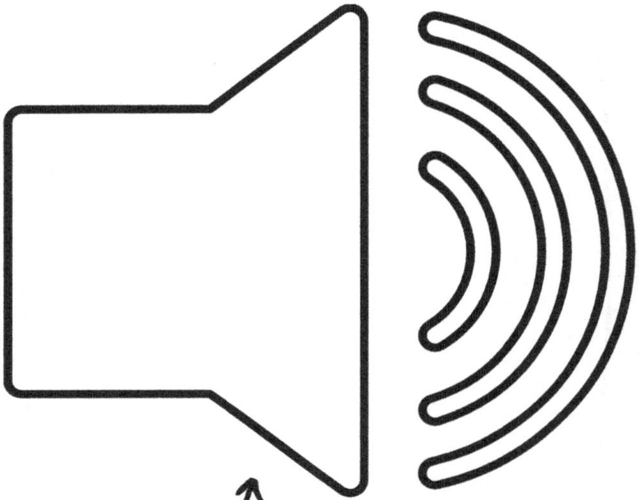

DRAW THEM HERE

DRAW OR WRITE HERE

RATE THE DAY

 **SOMETHING I AM THANKFUL FOR TODAY...**

_____

_____

_____

DAY: _____   **DATE:** ____ / ____ / ____

I HELPED SOMEONE TODAY WHEN...

A SKILL I AM THANKFUL FOR...

DRAW OR WRITE HERE

DRAW OR WRITE HERE

 **TODAY, I MOSTLY FELT...**

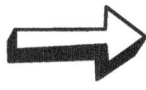 **TODAY, I AM MOST GRATEFUL FOR...**

_____

_____

_____

DAY: _____   DATE: ___ / ___ / ___

SOMETHING I WORKED HARD ON TODAY...

THE BEST THING ABOUT TECHNOLOGY IS...

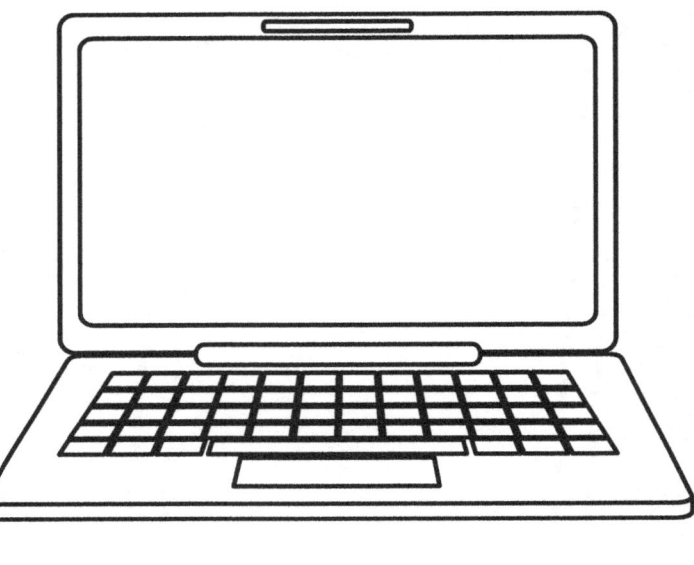

DRAW OR WRITE HERE

WHAT ARE YOU MOST THANKFUL FOR TODAY?

_____

_____

_____

_____

RATE THE DAY

← GREAT!

← OK

← NOT SO GREAT!

DAY: _____

DATE: _____ / _____ / _____

WHO MADE YOU FEEL CARED FOR TODAY?

WHAT I LOVE MOST ABOUT THE WEEKEND...

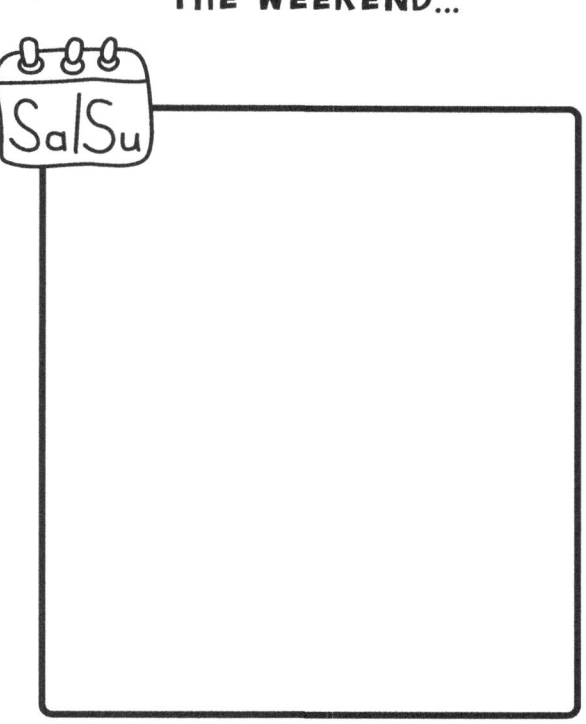

 DRAW THEM HERE

 RATE THE DAY

DRAW OR WRITE HERE

WHAT WERE YOU MOST GRATEFUL FOR THIS WEEK?

_____

_____

_____

DAY: _____   **DATE:** ____ / ____ / ____

I AM SO GRATEFUL I HAVE...

A PLACE I LOVE TO GO...

DRAW OR WRITE HERE

DRAW IT HERE

TODAY, I MOSTLY FELT...

☆ **SOMETHING I AM LOOKING FORWARD TO NEXT WEEK...** ☆

☆ _____ ☆

_____

☆ _____ ☆

DAY: _____   **DATE:** ____ / ____ / ____

I MADE SOMEONE FEEL HAPPY TODAY WHEN...

THE BEST THING ABOUT THIS TIME OF YEAR IS...

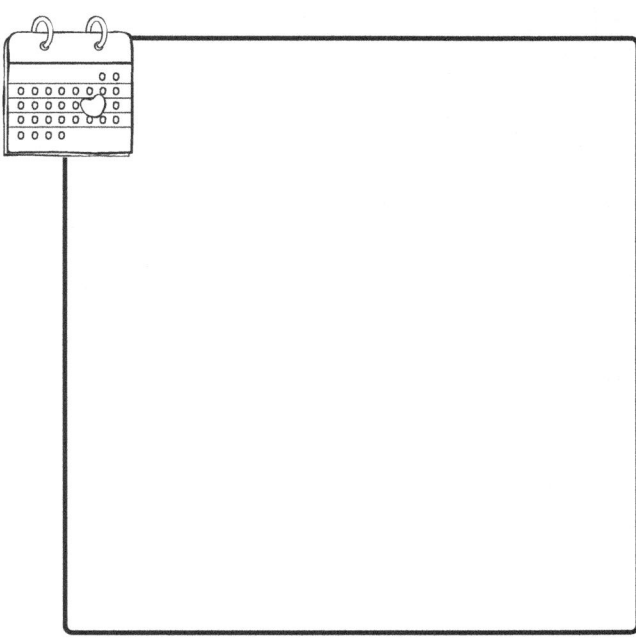

WHAT DID YOU DO?

TODAY, I MOSTLY FELT...

DRAW OR WRITE HERE

 **TODAY, I AM MOST THANKFUL FOR...**

_____

_____

_____

DAY: _____

DATE: _____ / _____ / _____

WHO LISTENED TO YOU TODAY?

SOMETHING IN NATURE I AM THANKFUL FOR...

DRAW THEM HERE

DRAW IT HERE

WHAT ARE YOU MOST GRATEFUL FOR TODAY?

_____

_____

_____

_____

RATE THE DAY

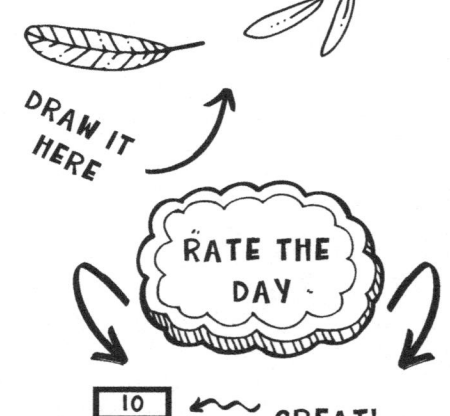

10	← GREAT!
9	
8	
7	
6	
5	← OK
4	
3	
2	
1	← NOT SO
0	← GREAT!

DAY: _____   DATE: ___/___/___

I LEARNED THIS
TODAY...

THE SINGER I AM MOST
GRATEFUL FOR...

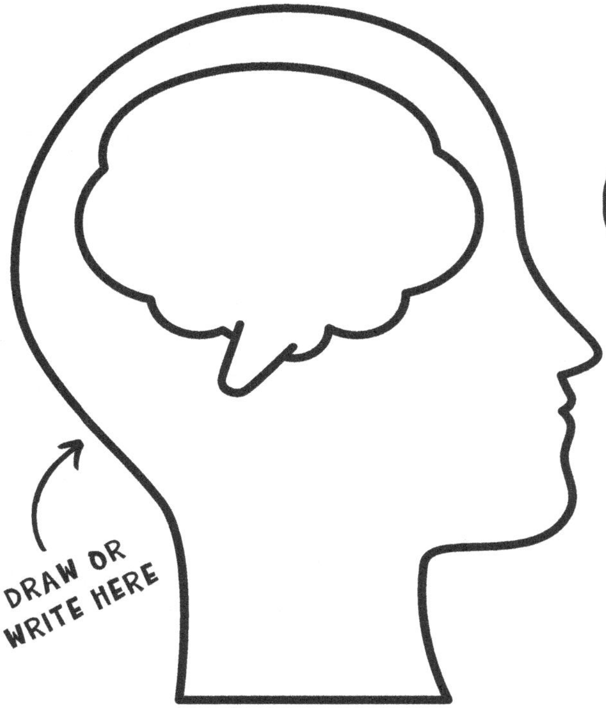

DRAW OR
WRITE HERE

DRAW OR
WRITE HERE

RATE THE
DAY

☆☆☆☆☆

 SOMETHING I AM THANKFUL FOR TODAY...

_____

_____

_____

DAY: _____   **DATE:** _____ / _____ / _____

SOMEONE WAS FRIENDLY TODAY WHEN...

SOMETHING I REALLY ENJOYED WATCHING TODAY...

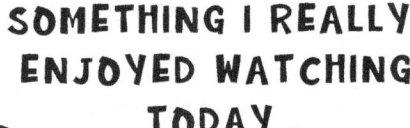

DRAW OR WRITE HERE

WHAT DID THEY DO?

TODAY, I MOSTLY FELT...

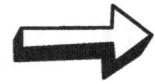

➡ TODAY, I AM MOST GRATEFUL FOR...

_____

_____

_____

DAY: _____   DATE: ___ / ___ / ___

I HAD A GREAT IDEA TODAY WHEN...

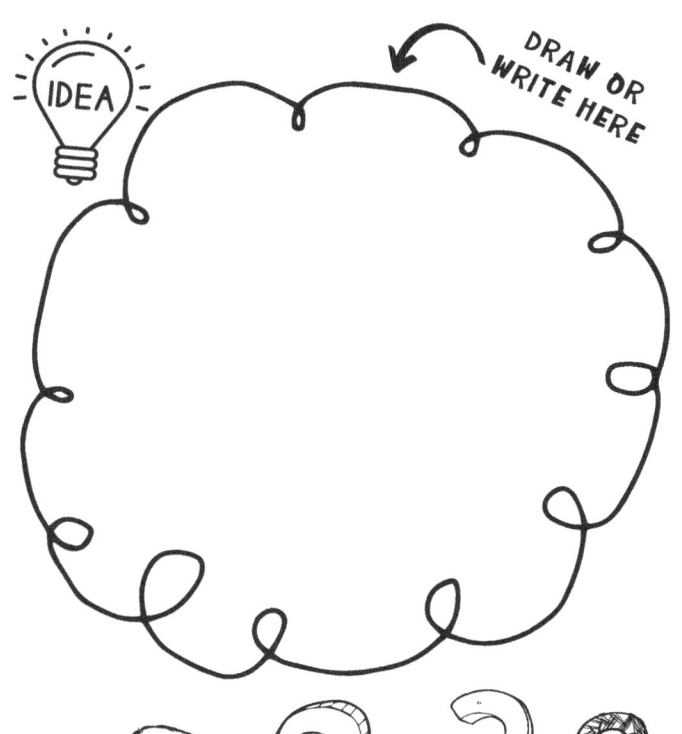

DRAW OR WRITE HERE

THE BEST THING ABOUT THE PLACE I LIVE IS...

DRAW OR WRITE HERE

WHAT ARE YOU MOST THANKFUL FOR TODAY?

_____

_____

_____

_____

RATE THE DAY

GREAT!

OK

NOT SO GREAT!

DAY: _____

DATE: ____ / ____ / ____

WHO MADE YOU FEEL LOVED TODAY?

SOMETHING BEAUTIFUL I AM THANKFUL FOR...

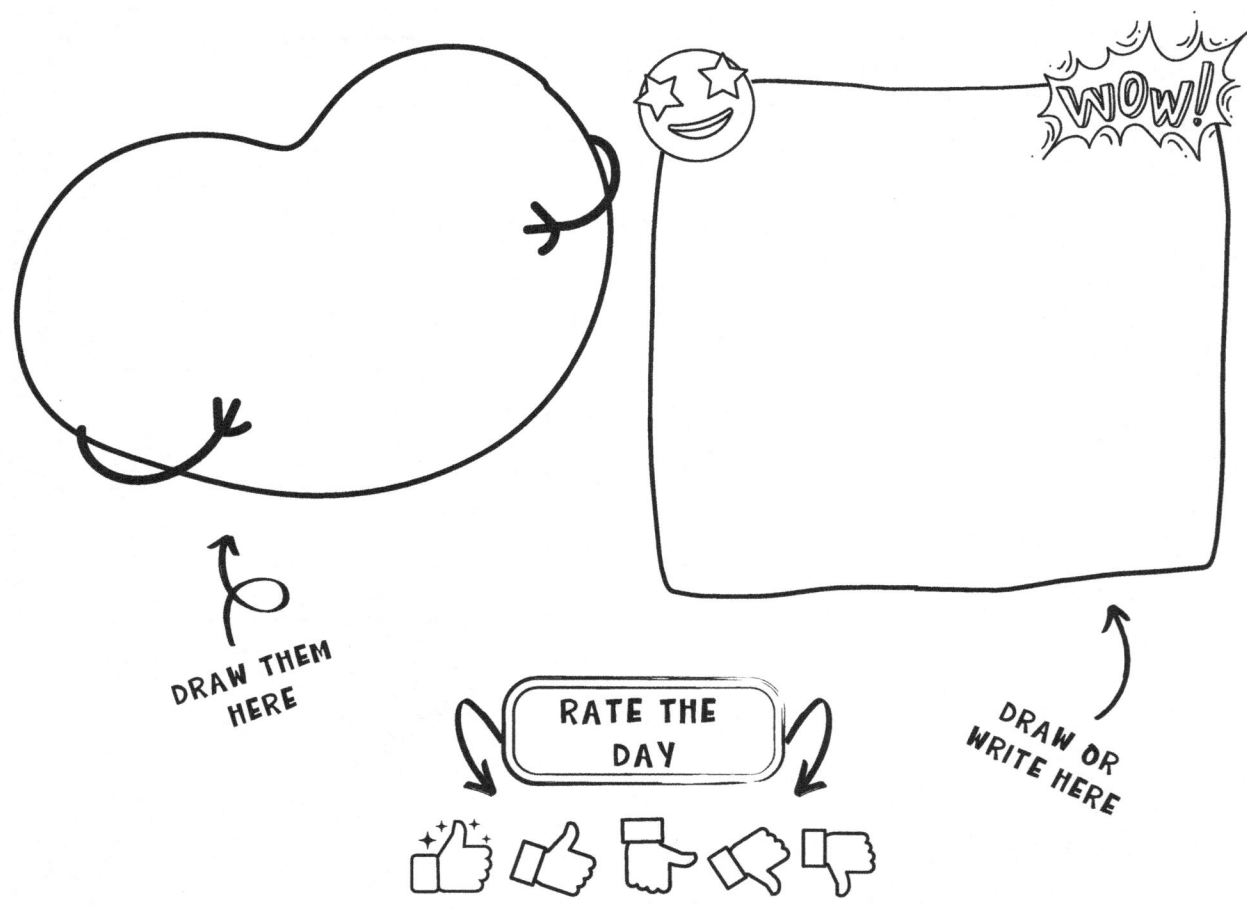

DRAW THEM HERE

RATE THE DAY

DRAW OR WRITE HERE

WHAT WERE YOU MOST GRATEFUL FOR THIS WEEK?

_____

_____

_____

DAY: _____

DATE: ____ / ____ / ____

I FELT RELAXED TODAY WHEN...

THE THING I LOVE MOST ABOUT MY HOME...

DRAW OR WRITE HERE

DRAW OR WRITE HERE

TODAY, I MOSTLY FELT...

☆ SOMETHING I AM LOOKING FORWARD TO NEXT WEEK... ☆

☆ _____ ☆

_____

☆ _____ ☆

DAY: _____   **DATE:** ___ / ___ / ___

I WAS KIND TODAY WHEN...

THE BEST THING THAT HAPPENED TO ME TODAY...

WHAT DID YOU DO?

DRAW OR WRITE HERE

TODAY, I MOSTLY FELT...

TODAY, I AM MOST THANKFUL FOR...

_____

_____

_____

DAY: _____ **DATE:** ___ / ___ / ___

I FELT CLEVER TODAY WHEN...

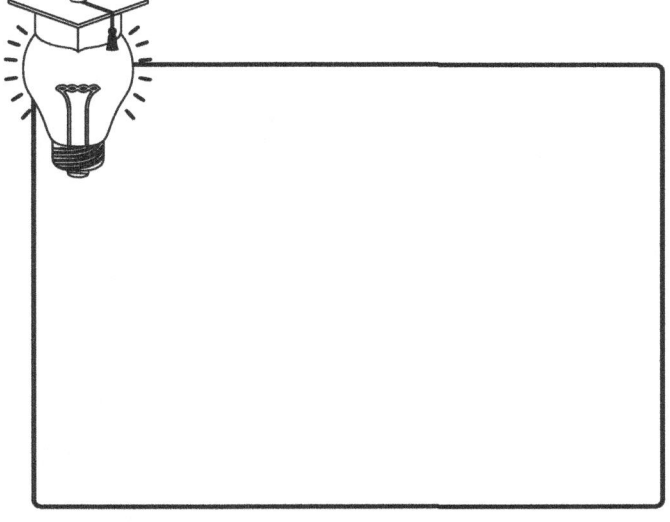

DRAW OR WRITE HERE

WHICH TEACHER ARE YOU MOST THANKFUL FOR TODAY?

DRAW THEM HERE

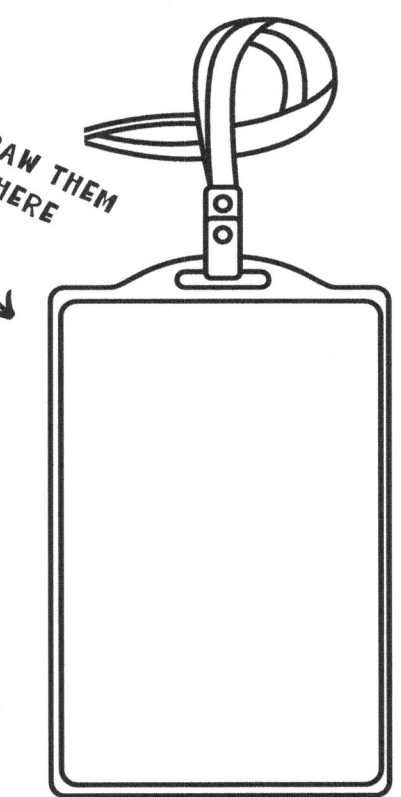

   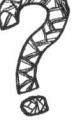 

WHAT ARE YOU MOST GRATEFUL FOR TODAY?

_____

_____

_____

_____

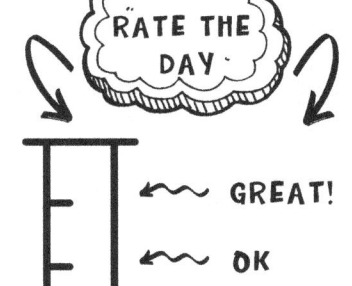

RATE THE DAY

GREAT!

OK

NOT SO GREAT!

DAY: _____

DATE: ___ / ___ / ___

WHO WAS YOUR HERO TODAY?

DRAW THEM HERE

THE CELEBRATION I LOVE THE MOST IS...

DRAW OR WRITE HERE

RATE THE DAY

SOMETHING I AM THANKFUL FOR TODAY...

_____

_____

_____

DAY: _____ **DATE:** ____ / ____ / ____

I ENJOYED SHARING TODAY WHEN...

THE BEST THING ABOUT MY COUNTRY IS...

DRAW OR WRITE HERE

DRAW OR WRITE HERE

TODAY, I MOSTLY FELT...

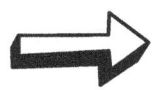 **TODAY, I AM MOST GRATEFUL FOR...**

_____

_____

_____

DAY: _____ DATE: ____ / ____ / ____

I WAS POLITE TODAY WHEN...

A COLD DRINK I AM GRATEFUL FOR...

DRAW OR WRITE HERE

WHAT DID YOU DO?

WHAT ARE YOU MOST THANKFUL FOR TODAY?

RATE THE DAY

_____

_____

_____

_____

← GREAT!

← OK

← NOT SO GREAT!

DAY: _____   **DATE:** ___ / ___ / ___

SOMEONE WHO ALWAYS HELPS ME...

A SPECIAL MEMORY I AM THANKFUL FOR...

DRAW OR WRITE HERE

DRAW THEM HERE

RATE THE DAY

WHAT WERE YOU MOST GRATEFUL FOR THIS WEEK?

_____

_____

_____

DAY: _____   DATE: _____ / _____ / _____

I AM REALLY GRATEFUL FOR MY...

THE BEST THING ABOUT BEING MY AGE IS...

DRAW OR WRITE HERE

DRAW OR WRITE HERE

TODAY, I MOSTLY FELT...

☆ SOMETHING I AM LOOKING FORWARD TO NEXT WEEK... ☆

☆ _____ ☆

_____

☆ _____ ☆

DAY: _____ **DATE:** ___ / ___ / ___

I MADE SOMEONE FEEL SPECIAL TODAY WHEN...

THE BEST THING ABOUT THE EVENING IS...

WHAT DID YOU DO?

DRAW OR WRITE HERE

TODAY, I MOSTLY FELT...

 **TODAY, I AM MOST THANKFUL FOR...**

_____

_____

_____

DAY: _____   DATE: ____ / ____ / ____

SOMETHING NICE SOMEONE
SAID TO ME
TODAY...

THE GAME I AM MOST
THANKFUL FOR...

WRITE WHAT
THEY SAID

DRAW IT
HERE

WHAT ARE YOU MOST
GRATEFUL FOR TODAY?

_____

_____

_____

_____

RATE THE
DAY

GREAT!

OK

NOT SO
GREAT!

DAY: _____   DATE: ____ / ____ / ____

I WAS GLAD TODAY WHEN...

SOMETHING OUTDOORS I AM GRATEFUL FOR...

WHAT HAPPENED?

RATE THE DAY

DRAW OR WRITE HERE

☆ ☆ ☆ ☆ ☆

 SOMETHING I AM THANKFUL FOR TODAY...

_____

_____

_____

DAY: _____   DATE: _____ / _____ / _____

I LOVED DOING THIS TODAY...

A MOVIE I AM GRATEFUL FOR...

DRAW OR WRITE HERE

DRAW OR WRITE HERE

TODAY, I MOSTLY FELT...

➡️ TODAY, I AM MOST GRATEFUL FOR...

_____

_____

_____

DAY: _____ **DATE:** ___ / ___ / ___

I WAS FRIENDLY TODAY WHEN...

WHAT DID YOU DO?

SOMETHING NEW I DID TODAY...

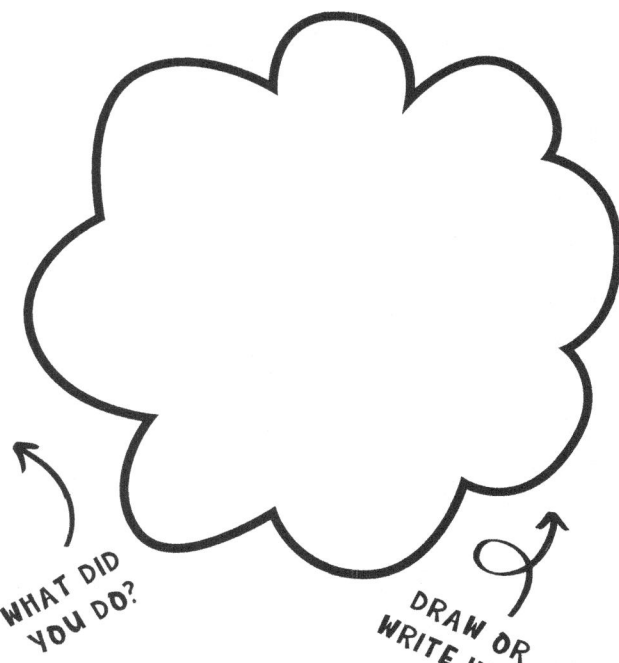

DRAW OR WRITE HERE

WHAT ARE YOU MOST THANKFUL FOR TODAY?

_____

_____

_____

_____

RATE THE DAY

10	← GREAT!
9	
8	
7	
6	
5	← OK
4	
3	
2	
1	← NOT SO
0	GREAT!

DAY: _____   DATE: ____ / ____ / ____

WHO PUT A SMILE ON YOUR
FACE TODAY?

THE BEST THING ABOUT
MY BODY IS...

DRAW THEM
HERE

RATE THE
DAY

DRAW OR
WRITE HERE

WHAT WERE YOU MOST GRATEFUL FOR THIS WEEK?

_____

_____

_____

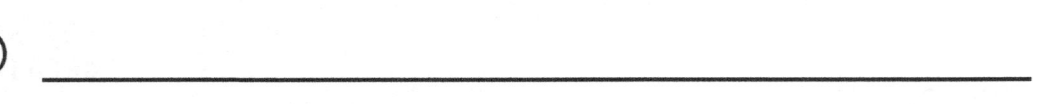

DAY: _____

DATE: ___ / ___ / ___

I HAD FUN TODAY WHEN...

WHAT HAPPENED?

SOMETHING IN MY ROOM I AM GRATEFUL FOR...

DRAW OR WRITE HERE

TODAY, I MOSTLY FELT...

☆ SOMETHING I AM LOOKING FORWARD TO NEXT WEEK... ☆

☆ _____

_____

☆ _____ ☆

DAY: _____ **DATE:** ____ / ____ / ____

THE BEST CONVERSATION I HAD TODAY...

A FRIEND I AM GRATEFUL FOR...

WRITE IT HERE

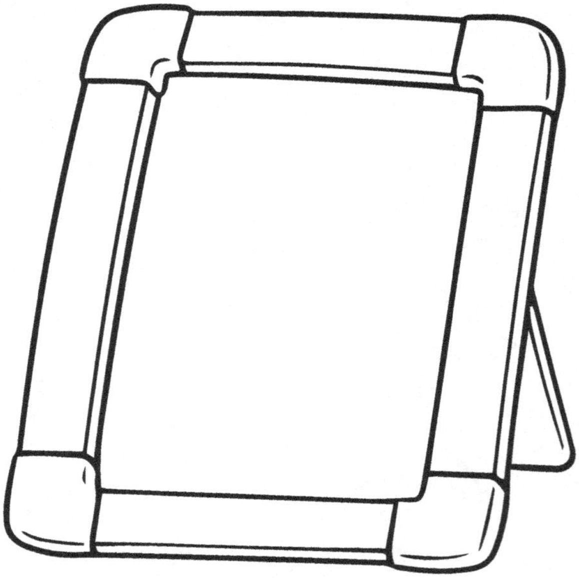

DRAW THEM HERE

TODAY, I MOSTLY FELT...

 TODAY, I AM MOST THANKFUL FOR...

_____

_____

_____

DAY: _____ **DATE:** _____ / _____ / _____

I WAS A STAR TODAY WHEN...

WHAT DID YOU DO?

DRAW OR WRITE HERE

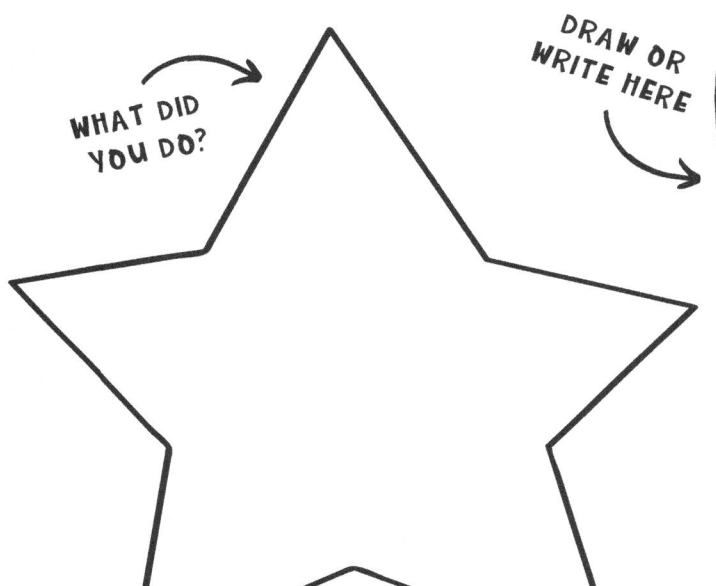

AN ACTIVITY I ENJOY DOING WITH OTHER PEOPLE...

WHAT ARE YOU MOST GRATEFUL FOR TODAY?

_____

_____

_____

_____

RATE THE DAY

GREAT!

OK

NOT SO GREAT!

DAY: _____   DATE: /   /

SOMEONE WAS HELPFUL TODAY WHEN...

A PHOTO THAT IS SPECIAL TO ME...

WHAT DID THEY DO?

RATE THE DAY

DRAW IT HERE

SOMETHING I AM THANKFUL FOR TODAY...

_____

_____

_____

DAY: _____   **DATE:** ___ / ___ / ___

SOMETHING THOUGHTFUL I SAID TO SOMEONE TODAY...

THE HOLIDAY I AM MOST THANKFUL FOR...

WHAT DID YOU SAY?

DRAW OR WRITE HERE

TODAY, I MOSTLY FELT...

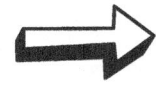 **TODAY, I AM MOST GRATEFUL FOR...**

_____

_____

_____

DAY: _____   **DATE:** _____ / _____ / _____

I FELT GREAT TODAY WHEN...

DRAW WHAT HAPPENED

A GIFT I REALLY ENJOYED GIVING...

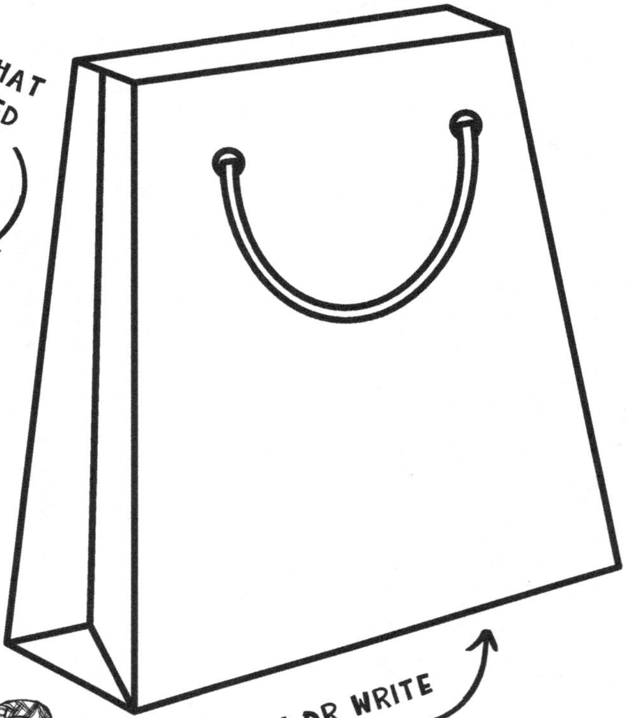

DRAW OR WRITE HERE

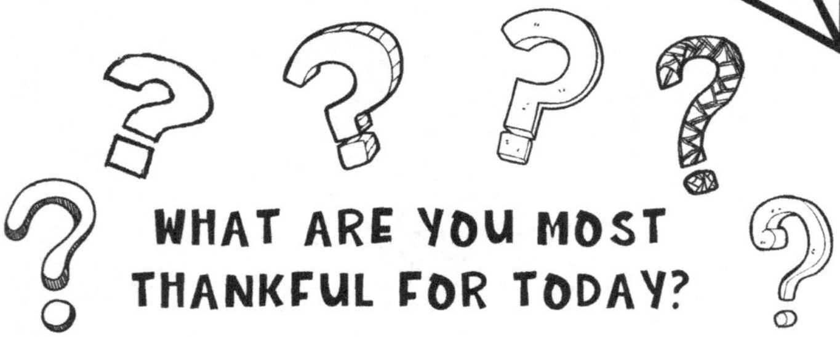

WHAT ARE YOU MOST THANKFUL FOR TODAY?

_____

_____

_____

_____

RATE THE DAY

~ GREAT!

~ OK

~ NOT SO GREAT!

DAY: _____   **DATE:** _____ / _____ / _____

SOMEONE WHO CARES FOR ME...

SOMETHING I ENJOY DOING OUTDOORS...

DRAW THEM HERE

DRAW OR WRITE HERE

RATE THE DAY

WHAT WERE YOU MOST GRATEFUL FOR THIS WEEK?

_____

_____

_____

DAY: _____   DATE: ____ / ____ / ____

I AM GRATEFUL I LEARNED HOW TO...

THE BEST THING ABOUT BEING ME IS...

DRAW OR WRITE HERE

TODAY, I MOSTLY FELT...

DRAW OR WRITE HERE

☆ SOMETHING I AM LOOKING FORWARD TO NEXT WEEK... ☆

☆ _____
_____ ☆

☆ _____ ☆

DAY: _____   DATE: _____ / _____ / _____

I CHEERED SOMEONE UP
TODAY WHEN...

THE TIME OF DAY I AM
MOST THANKFUL FOR...

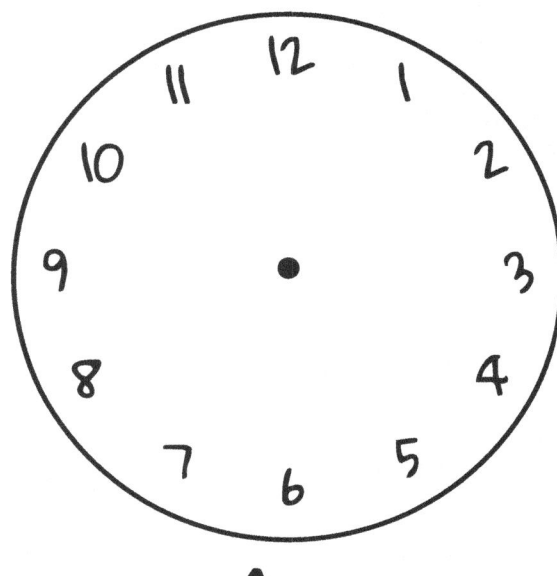

WHAT DID YOU DO?

DRAW IT HERE

TODAY, I MOSTLY FELT...

TODAY, I AM MOST THANKFUL FOR...

_____

_____

_____

DAY: _____

DATE: _____ / _____ / _____

SOMETHING KIND SOMEONE
DID FOR ME TODAY...

THE THING I LOVE MOST
ABOUT MY LIFE...

WHAT DID
THEY DO?

DRAW OR
WRITE HERE

WHAT ARE YOU MOST
GRATEFUL FOR TODAY?

RATE THE
DAY

_____

_____

_____

_____

GREAT!

OK

NOT SO
GREAT!

DAY: _____

DATE: ___ / ___ / ___

A TIME I FELT PROUD OF MYSELF...

THE SEASON I AM MOST GRATEFUL FOR...

WHAT DID YOU DO?

RATE THE DAY

☆☆☆☆☆

DRAW OR WRITE HERE

 SOMETHING I AM THANKFUL FOR TODAY...

_____

_____

_____

DAY: _____   DATE: ___ / ___ / ___

TODAY'S AWARD FOR BRAVERY GOES TO...

A SPECIAL PLACE I AM THANKFUL FOR...

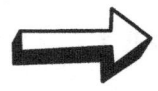 DRAW OR WRITE HERE

DRAW OR WRITE HERE

TODAY, I MOSTLY FELT...

TODAY, I AM MOST GRATEFUL FOR...

_____

_____

_____

DAY: _____   DATE: ___/___/___

I HELPED SOMEONE
TODAY WHEN I SAID...

SOMETHING I AM GOOD AT
THAT I AM GRATEFUL FOR...

WRITE HERE

DRAW OR
WRITE HERE

WHAT ARE YOU MOST
THANKFUL FOR TODAY?

RATE THE
DAY

GREAT!

OK

NOT SO
GREAT!

DAY: _____   **DATE:** ____ / ____ / ____

WHO MADE YOU LAUGH TODAY?

HA HA

A HOT DRINK I AM GRATEFUL FOR...

DRAW THEM HERE

RATE THE DAY

DRAW OR WRITE HERE

WHAT WERE YOU MOST GRATEFUL FOR THIS WEEK?

_____

_____

_____

DAY: _____   **DATE:** ___ / ___ / ___

I FELT POSITIVE TODAY WHEN...

WHICH PART OF YOUR BODY ARE YOU MOST GRATEFUL FOR?

WHAT HAPPENED?

DRAW OR WRITE HERE

TODAY, I MOSTLY FELT...

☆ **SOMETHING I AM LOOKING FORWARD TO NEXT WEEK...** ☆

☆ _____

_____

☆ _____ ☆

DAY: _____   DATE: /   /

SOMETHING NICE I DID FOR
SOMEONE TODAY...

AN ACTIVITY I ENJOY
DOING ON MY OWN...

WHAT
DID YOU DO?

TODAY, I MOSTLY FELT...

DRAW OR
WRITE HERE

TODAY, I AM MOST THANKFUL FOR...

_____

_____

_____

DAY: _____

DATE: ___ / ___ / ___

I WAS PLEASED TODAY WHEN...

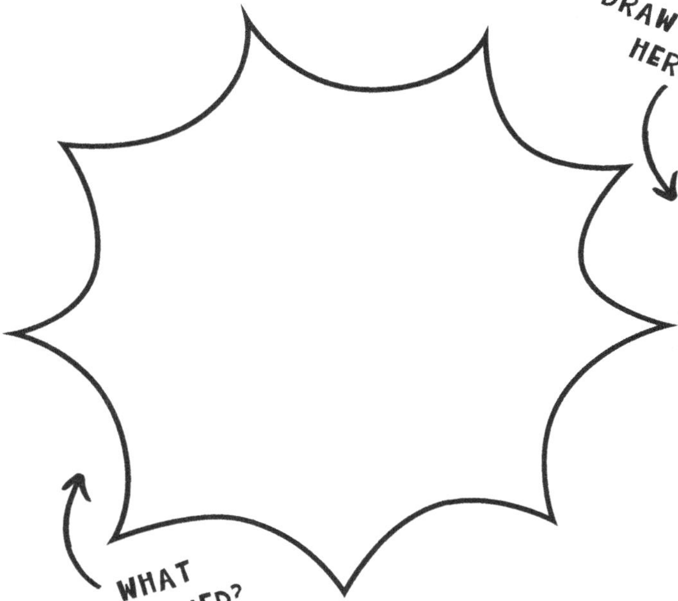

A SPECIAL PERSON I AM THANKFUL FOR...

DRAW THEM HERE

WHAT HAPPENED?

WHAT ARE YOU MOST GRATEFUL FOR TODAY?

_____

_____

_____

_____

RATE THE DAY

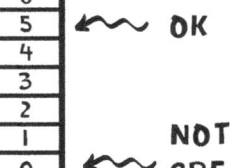

10	GREAT!
9	
8	
7	
6	
5	OK
4	
3	
2	
1	NOT SO
0	GREAT!

DAY: _____ **DATE:** ____ / ____ / ____

WHO HELPED YOU TODAY?

THE NICEST MESSAGE I EVER RECEIVED...

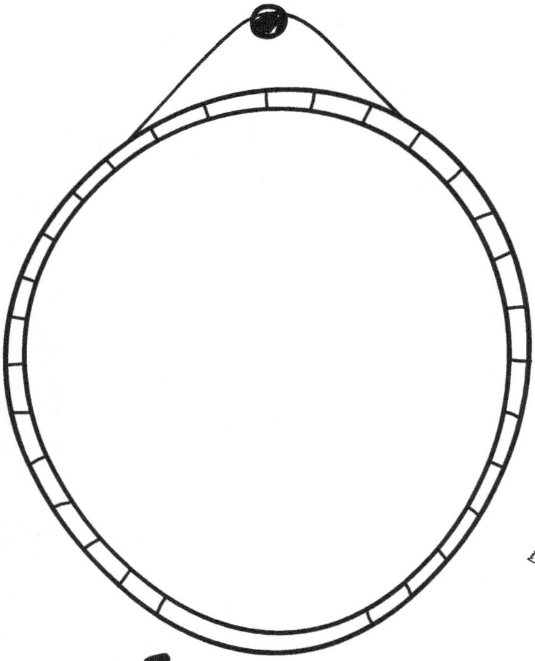

DRAW THEM HERE

WRITE IT HERE

RATE THE DAY

 **SOMETHING I AM THANKFUL FOR TODAY...**

_____

_____

_____

DAY: _____   DATE: _____ / _____ / _____

SOMEONE WHO MAKES
MY LIFE BETTER...

AN ITEM THAT IS
SPECIAL TO ME...

DRAW THEM
HERE

TODAY, I MOSTLY FELT...

DRAW OR
WRITE HERE

TODAY, I AM MOST GRATEFUL FOR...

_____

_____

_____

DAY: _____

DATE: ____ / ____ / ____

SOMETHING I WAS REALLY GOOD AT TODAY...

DRAW WHAT YOU DID

SOMEWHERE I LIKE TO VISIT THAT I AM GRATEFUL FOR...

DRAW OR WRITE HERE

 **WHAT ARE YOU MOST THANKFUL FOR TODAY?**

_____

_____

_____

_____

 RATE THE DAY

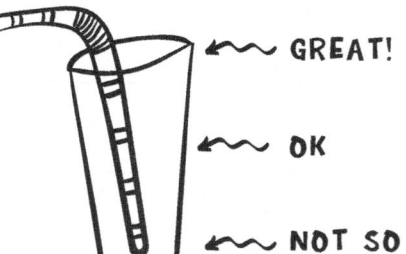
← GREAT!

← OK

← NOT SO GREAT!

DAY: _____   **DATE:** ____ / ____ / ____

SOMETHING FUNNY SOMEONE SAID TO ME TODAY...

THE THING I LOVE MOST ABOUT MY FACE...

WHAT DID THEY SAY?

DRAW OR WRITE HERE

RATE THE DAY

WHAT WERE YOU MOST GRATEFUL FOR THIS WEEK?

_____

_____

_____

DAY: _____   DATE: ___ / ___ / ___

I MADE SOMEONE FEEL LOVED TODAY WHEN...

THE BEST DREAM I EVER HAD...

WHAT DID YOU DO?

DRAW OR WRITE HERE

z z Z

TODAY, I MOSTLY FELT...

⭐ **SOMETHING I AM LOOKING FORWARD TO NEXT WEEK...** ⭐

⭐ _____ ⭐

_____

⭐ _____ ⭐

DAY: _____ **DATE:** _____ / _____ / _____

SOMETHING KIND I DID FOR SOMEONE TODAY...

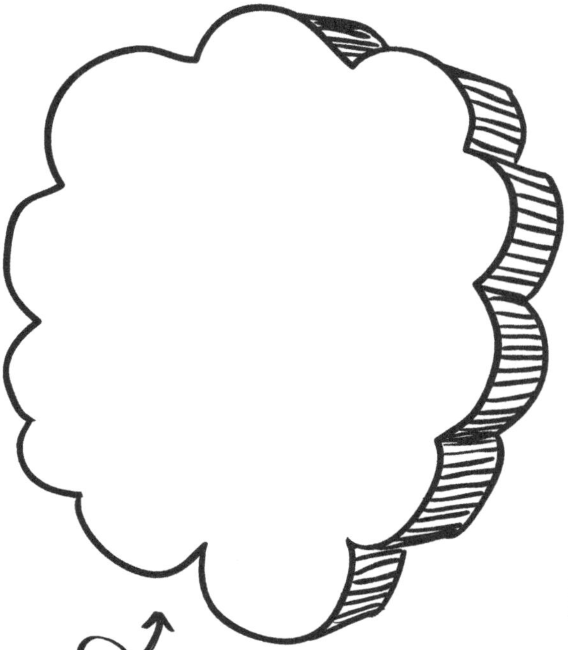

MY PERFECT DAY WOULD BE SPENT...

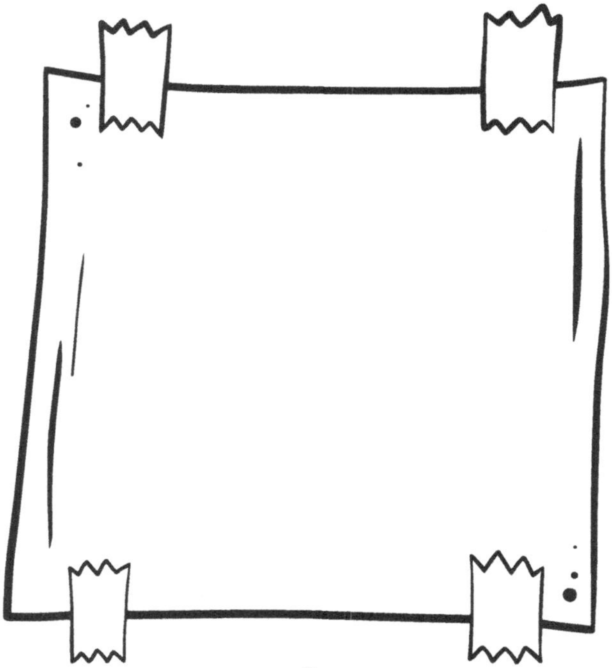

WHAT DID YOU DO?

DRAW OR WRITE HERE

TODAY, I MOSTLY FELT...

 **TODAY, I AM MOST THANKFUL FOR...**

_____

_____

_____

DAY: _____ **DATE:** ___ / ___ / ___

WHO WAS A GOOD FRIEND TODAY?

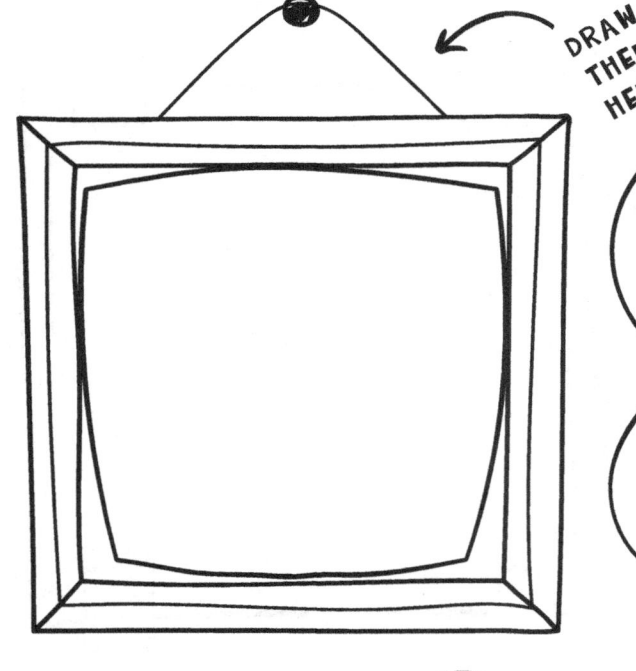

DRAW THEM HERE

SOMEWHERE I LOVE TO CHILL OUT...

DRAW OR WRITE HERE

WHAT ARE YOU MOST GRATEFUL FOR TODAY?

_____

_____

_____

_____

RATE THE DAY

GREAT!

OK

NOT SO GREAT!

DAY: _____   **DATE:** ____ / ____ / ____

SOMEONE I LOOK UP TO...

DRAW THEM HERE

SOMETHING I FOUND DIFFICULT, BUT I DID IT ANYWAY...

DRAW OR WRITE HERE

RATE THE DAY

☆ ☆ ☆ ☆ ☆

 **SOMETHING I AM THANKFUL FOR TODAY...**

_____

_____

_____

DAY: _____ **DATE:** ___ / ___ / ___

SOMETHING THOUGHTFUL SOMEONE SAID TO ME TODAY...

THE BEST THING ABOUT THE SCHOOL HOLIDAYS IS...

HAPPY HOLIDAYS

WHAT DID THEY SAY?

DRAW OR WRITE HERE

TODAY, I MOSTLY FELT...

TODAY, I AM MOST GRATEFUL FOR...

_____

_____

_____

DAY: _____   DATE: ___ / ___ / ___

SOMETHING PEOPLE
LOVE ABOUT ME...   WHAT'S ITS
                          NAME?

A SHOP I AM
GRATEFUL FOR...

DRAW OR
WRITE HERE

WHAT ARE YOU MOST
THANKFUL FOR TODAY?

RATE THE
DAY

_____

_____

_____

_____

GREAT!

OK

NOT SO
GREAT!

DAY: _____   DATE: ___ / ___ / ___

SOMEONE WHO ALWAYS
CHEERS ME UP...

SOMETHING THAT MAKES
ME FEEL SAFE...

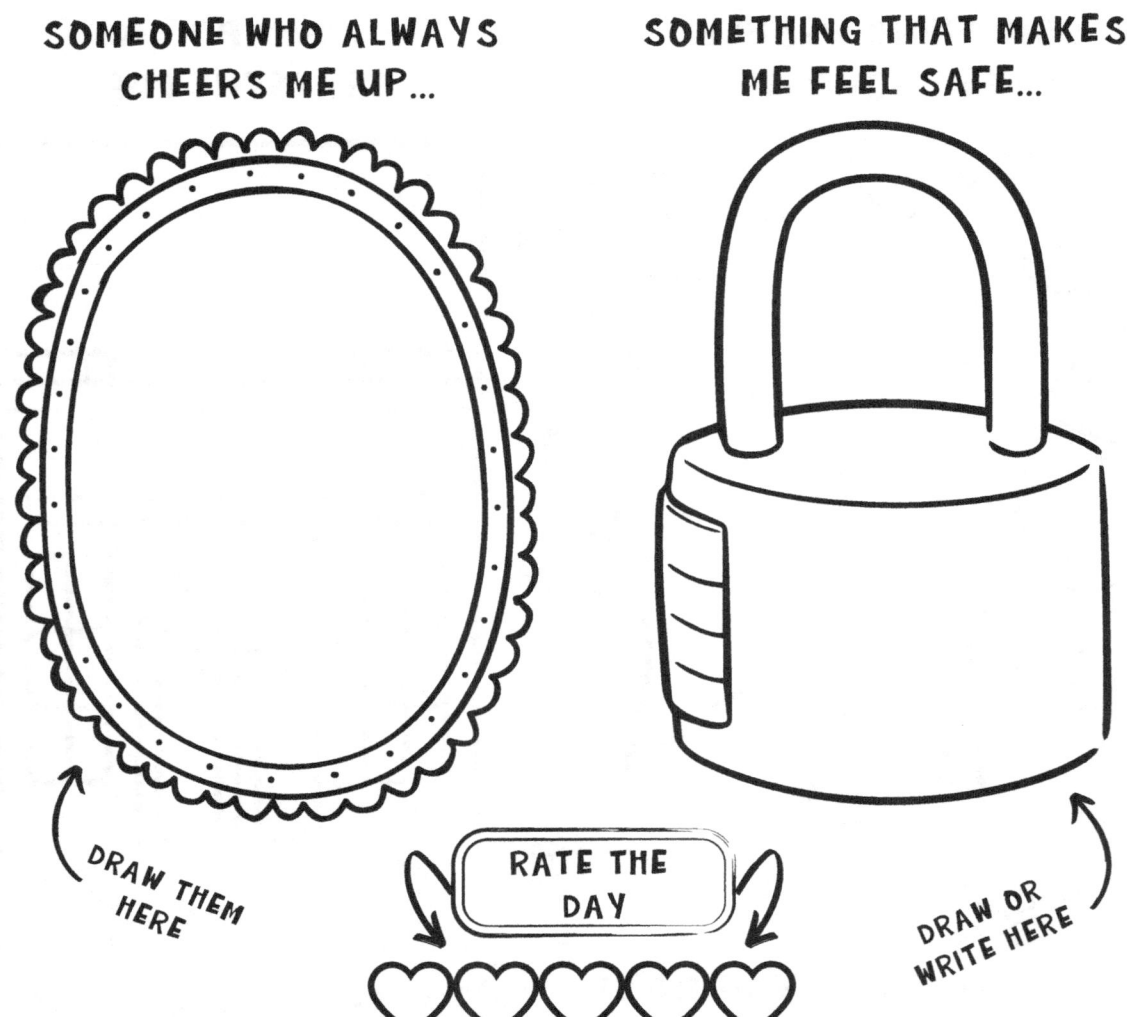

DRAW THEM
HERE

RATE THE
DAY

DRAW OR
WRITE HERE

WHAT WERE YOU MOST GRATEFUL FOR THIS WEEK?

_____

_____

_____

DAY: _____ **DATE:** _____ / _____ / _____

I FELT CALM TODAY WHEN...

A HOUSEHOLD OBJECT I AM GRATEFUL FOR...

DRAW OR WRITE HERE

DRAW OR WRITE HERE

TODAY, I MOSTLY FELT...

☆ SOMETHING I AM LOOKING FORWARD TO NEXT WEEK... ☆

☆ _____ ☆

_____

☆ _____ ☆

DAY: _____   DATE: /   /

SOMETHING THOUGHTFUL I DID FOR SOMEONE TODAY...

WHAT SMELL ARE YOU MOST GRATEFUL FOR?

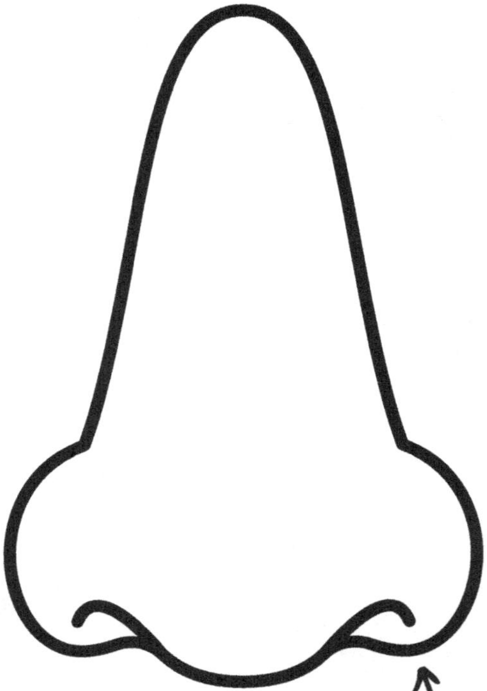

WHAT DID YOU DO?

TODAY, I MOSTLY FELT...

DRAW OR WRITE HERE

 TODAY, I AM MOST THANKFUL FOR...

_____

_____

_____

DAY: _____   DATE: ___/___/___

I WAS A HERO TODAY WHEN...

WHAT DID YOU DO?

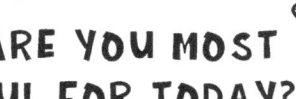
WHAT ARE YOU MOST GRATEFUL FOR TODAY?

_____

_____

_____

_____

SOMETHING INDOORS I AM THANKFUL FOR...

DRAW OR WRITE HERE

RATE THE DAY

GREAT!

OK

NOT SO GREAT!

DAY: _____   **DATE:** ____ / ____ / ____

SOMEONE HELPED ME TODAY WHEN THEY SAID...

THE ADULT I AM MOST GRATEFUL FOR TODAY...

WHAT DID THEY SAY?

DRAW THEM HERE

RATE THE DAY

SOMETHING I AM THANKFUL FOR TODAY...

_____

_____

_____

DAY: _____   DATE: ____ / ____ / ____

I AM A GOOD FRIEND
BECAUSE...

SOMETHING I AM THANKFUL
FOR THAT DOESN'T COST
ANY MONEY...

FREE

DRAW OR
WRITE HERE

DRAW OR
WRITE HERE

TODAY, I MOSTLY FELT...

TODAY, I AM MOST GRATEFUL FOR...

_____

_____

_____

DAY: _____   **DATE:** ___ / ___ / ___

SOMETHING I DID REALLY WELL TODAY...

WHAT DID YOU DO?

MY FAVOURITE PLACE TO EAT IS...

DRAW OR WRITE HERE

WHAT ARE YOU MOST THANKFUL FOR TODAY?

_____

_____

_____

_____

RATE THE DAY

| 10 |
| 9 |
| 8 |
| 7 |
| 6 |
| 5 |
| 4 |
| 3 |
| 2 |
| 1 |
| 0 |

← GREAT!

← OK

← NOT SO GREAT!

DAY: _____   DATE: _____ / _____ / _____

SOMEONE WHO ALWAYS MAKES ME SMILE...   **THE BEST THING ABOUT MY FAMILY IS...**

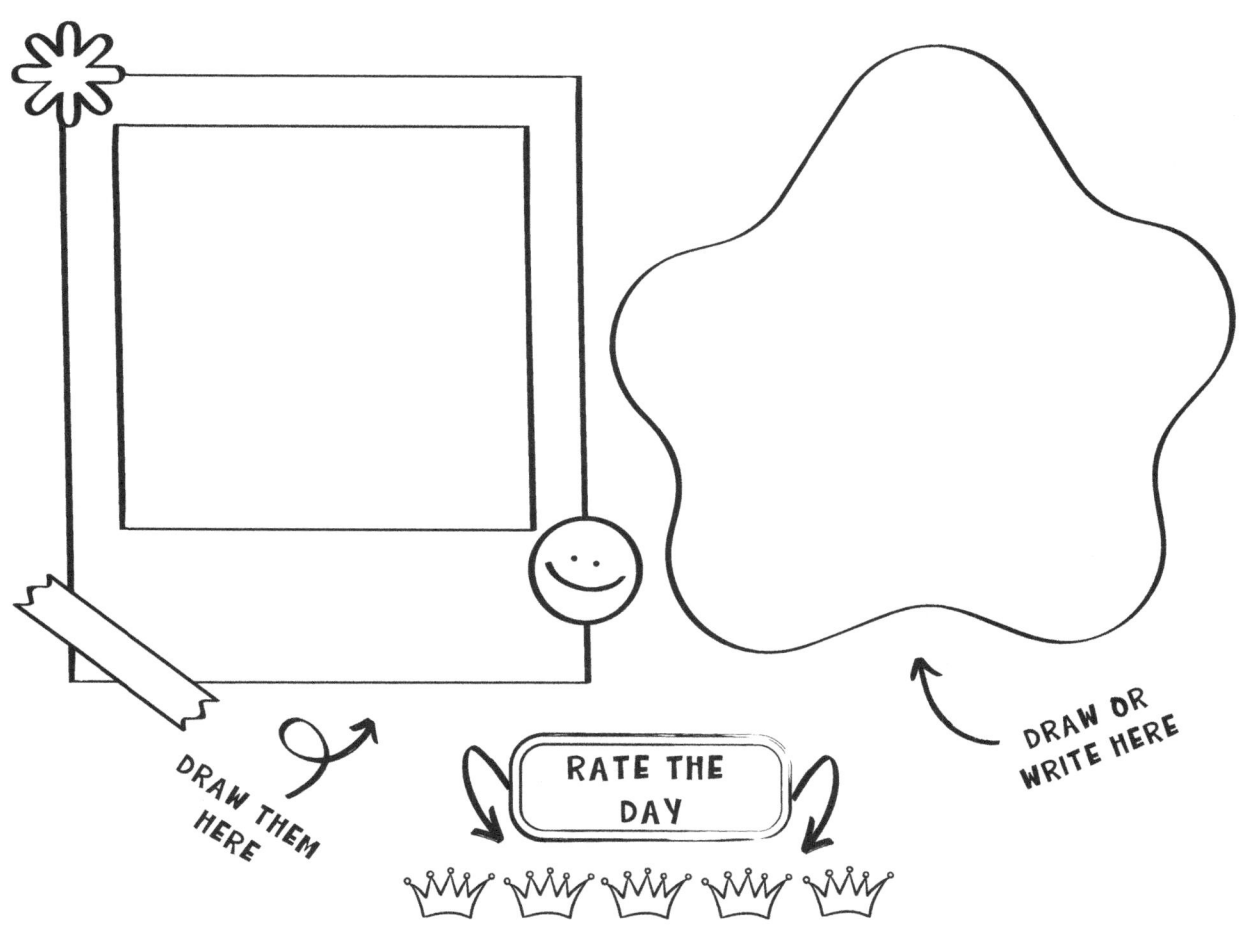

DRAW THEM HERE

RATE THE DAY

DRAW OR WRITE HERE

WHAT WERE YOU MOST GRATEFUL FOR THIS WEEK?

_____

_____

_____

DAY: _____   DATE: ___ / ___ / ___

I WAS A BRILLIANT ROLE MODEL TODAY WHEN...

THE MOMENT I AM MOST GRATEFUL FOR TODAY...

WHAT DID YOU DO?

TODAY, I MOSTLY FELT...

DRAW OR WRITE HERE

 SOMETHING I AM LOOKING FORWARD TO NEXT WEEK...

 _____

_____

 _____

Made in the USA
Monee, IL
18 August 2022

11899733R00057